ADVENTURES OF SHERLOCK HOLMES

Plays written by

Rina Rachel Sondhi

FOR THE CHILDREN OF ORVIETO

The Project

The British School of Orvieto worked in Partnership with The Scuola Media Orvieto and Baschi to develop the students' acquisition of the English Language through a series of short plays. The plays introduced a series of simple and complex sentences using key vocabulary to engage the students and to develop their confidence to speak English.

The Plays were written according to the ability and age of the students to develop their understanding of English humour and a variety of Language techniques.

The scripts are designed for individual lessons and can be used for assemblies and small-scale productions. The theme of Sherlock Holmes was introduced throughout the plays to inspire the students and engage them in a 'fun' way.

PLAYS

Written by Rina Sondhi

Scuola Media Robbery Act 1

Scuola Media Robbery Act 2

SHERLOCK AND the CASE of the Mummy

Sherlock Holmes and the Space Detectives

Sherlock Holmes and the Monster of Orvieto -

Sherlock Holmes in the Playground

SHERLOCK AND CAPITANO DEL POPOLO

Treasure on Bolsena ISLAND

Red Riding Hood Meets Sherlock Holmes

The Scuola Media Robbery

Cast: teacher   school children   Moriarty robbers   2,3,4,5,6, Sherlock Holmes Dr Watson Sherlock Holmes

Scene 1:   In the classroom.

Child: The teacher is coming; the teacher is coming.

Sound effects.   Door Opening. footsteps

Teacher: Good morning everyone, I am the new teacher. How are you?

Children: Fine thank you, and you?

Child (*desperately puts their hand up*): Can I go to the toilet?

Teacher: No
Child (*desperately puts their hand up*): Can I go to the toilet?

Teacher: No
Child (*desperately puts their hand up*): Can I go to the toilet?

Teacher: I said No – you will have to wait till Break time!

Child 2 :   What are we going to learn today?

Teacher :   We are going to learn about Nouns, Verbs and Adjectives

Child 1 :   What is an adjective? Is it something that describes the Noun?

Teacher :   Yes – well done.

Sound Effects   : The school bell rings-   ding- a - ling - a- ling.

Children: Hooray….Hooray….

Sound Effects : Door opening ; Children running

Scene 2

ACTION Robbers enter on tiptoes in a line – smallest to tallest. They cross the class then the first one stops and the next one bumps into the first etc. Then then robbers make a line facing the audience.

Robbers: Hello everyone. We are strong, we are clever, we are bad. We are robbers!

(creating hand gestures for Strong, Clever, bad and robbers)

ACTION The robbers go round the class pointing to objects.

Moriarty :   What's this?
Robber 2:   It's a Blue pen?
Robber 3:   What's this?
Robber 4:   It's a Yellow chair.

Robber 5:   What's this?

Robber 6:   It's a waste bin full of trash

Robber: 1:   What's this?

Robber 2:   It's a bag. In fact, it is a back pack!

Moriarty :   A back pack! Quick Take ALL the bags including Back Packs

ACTION The robbers pick up the bags and move towards the door. They are about to exit when a robber sees the children (offstage)

Robbers: Oh no, the children are coming. Quick hide behind the yellow chair

ACTION The robbers hide behind the chairs, or in the corner. Children enter and notice the bags have gone

Children: Where are the bags? Where are the bags? Where are our Back packs?

Child: Quick Call the police!

Sound effects : A child calls the police. Police car sound

Child: Police, come quickly. There are robbers at the Scuola Media

Sound Effects : Sound of police siren off stage. The police arrive, running. The run into the class and stop

Sherlock Holmes :   Don't panic. Don't panic! We are the police. We are strong, we are clever, we are ….. the Super Investigators. What is the problem?

Children: There are robbers. They have stolen our Back packs

ACTION They all start looking for the robbers.

Moriarty: Atchoo!

Children: What was that?

Dr Watson: I don't know. It sounds familiar.

Moriarty: Atchoo!

Children: What's that?

Sherlock Holmes: I don't know but I have heard that sound before…

Sound effects : Sneezing sounds

Moriarty: Atchoo!

Children: Look! It´s the robbers! They are behind the yellow chairs

ACTION The children and police chase the robbers. Everyone runs in a circle 3 times until a robber says Hands up!

Robbers: Hands up!

ACTION The children and police move to the side

Children, Police: Oh no!

Robbers: You cannot stop us. We are strong, we are clever, we are bad. We are robbers!

Sherlock and Watson: More like Moriarty and his band of merry Robbers!!!

Look! What's that?

ACTION : The robbers all turn around to look, and Sherlock and Watson catch them and arrest them.

Everyone: Hooray, hooray!

Children: Thank you Sherlock Holmes

Sherlock and Watson: You're welcome

Watson: You did it again Sherlock – how do you do it?

Sherlock Holmes : It is Elementary my dear Watson, Elementary!!

The Scuola Media Robbery ACT 2

Cast: teacher school children Moriarty robbers 2,3,4,5,6, Sherlock Holmes Dr Watson Lady Aquila

Scene 1: In the classroom.

Child: The teacher is coming; the teacher is coming.

Sound effects.   Door Opening. footsteps

Teacher: Good morning everyone, how are you? I hope everyone is feeling excited.

Children: Yes, we are Fine thanking you and we are very excited today!

Child 1 (*desperately puts their hand up*): Can I go to the toilet?

Teacher: No

Child (*desperately puts their hand up*): Can I go to the toilet?

Teacher: No

Child 1 (*desperately puts their hand up*): Can I go to the toilet?

Teacher: I said No – you will have to wait till lunchtime!

Child 2 : What are we going to learn today?

Teacher : Today we are going to learn about Mysteries, in fact "How to solve a mystery."

Child 3 : Do you mean like Mysteries that the great Sherlock Holmes solves?

Teacher : Yes, absolutely right. Do you remember the Robbery we had last year?

Child 1 : Yes, the one where the robbers came into our classroom and stole our backpacks?

Narrator : There is a FLASHBACK

ACTION Robbers enter on tiptoes in a line. They cross the class then the first one stops and the next one bumps into the first etc. Then then robbers make a line facing the audience.

Robbers: Hello everyone. We are strong, we are clever, we are bad. We are robbers!

ACTION The robbers go round the class pointing to objects.

Moriarty : What's this?
Robber 2: It's a Blue pen?
Robber 3: What's this?
Robber 4: It's a Yellow chair.
Robber 5: What's this?

Robber 6: It´s a waste bin full of trash

Robber: 1: What's this?
Robber 2: It´s a bag. In fact, it is a back pack!
Moriarty : A back pack! Quick Take ALL the bags including Back Packs

ACTION The robbers pick up the bags and move towards the door. They are about to exit when a robber sees the children (offstage)

Robbers: Oh no, the children are coming. Quick hide behind the yellow chair

ACTION The robbers hide behind the chairs, or in the corner. Children enter and notice the bags have gone

Narrator : RETURNING TO THE PRESERNT

Children: Ah yes We remember – they stole so many things…
Child 1: Yes , but Sherlock Holmes and Watson saved the day.
Child 2 : They tricked the Robbers by distracting them.
Child 3 : They really are super investigators

Teacher : Let's watch a scene from one of his amazing Plays :

"Sherlock Holmes & The mystery of the Aquila diamond:

Narrator: The story begins inside 221B Baker St. Holmes and Watson are sitting by the fire playing chess. There is a knock at the door.

Holmes: Get that would you Watson.

Watson: Certainly Holmes (goes to the door, opens it, in bursts a woman in very expensive riding gear, boots and a riding hat perched on top of a large nest-like hairdo) Good- ness me!

Lady Aquila: Mr. Holmes (addressing Watson) I need to speak with you immediately! It is of the utmost importance!

Watson: Well I never.... Goodness me!

Holmes: (coolly, without turning round) And Mr. Sherlock Holmes will speak to you when he decides that he is good and ready!

Lady Aquila: And who might you be Sir!

Holmes: (getting up and turning round) I, Madame, might be Mr. Sherlock Holmes. In fact, I definitely was the last time I looked! And you, you are Lady Henrietta Aquila of Porkington. You have rushed here, directly from riding in the hunt to ask me to re- cover the famous Aquila Diamond which was, two days ago, stolen from your country house!

Watson: Goodness me! Jolly good show Holmes!

Lady Aquila: (astonished) How on earth did you know all that Mr. Holmes? I haven't breathed a word to anyone!

Watson: It's just a talent that he has. But I'd like to know anyway.

Holmes: Elementary, my dear Watson, elementary. First, the knock on the door. Too loud for a hand, but not for the ornate silver riding crop that her Ladyship is holding. As for coming straight from the hunt, well, leather riding boots, fresh mud, and the un- mistakable smell of horse manure, simple really.

Lady Aquila: But my name! And about the diamond.

Holmes: Quite straight forward! You have a ridiculously expensive hairdo covered by an ex- tremely sad hat, and your picture is in tonight's paper under the headline "Famous Aquila diamond stolen from Lady Aquila". It is this that has brought you in such a fervour and so quickly to 221b Baker St!

Watson: Marvelous! I told you he was a smarty pants! Good show Holmes!

Lady Aquila: Yes, Yes! Very clever!

Narrator : Back in the classroom

Children :   WOW That was fantastic – So much information

Sound Effects : Sound of police siren off stage. Sherlock Holmes and Watson arrive, running. They run into the class and stop.

Sherlock Holmes :   Don't panic. Don't panic! We are strong, we are clever, we are ….. the Super Investigators. And WE ARE BACK!

Children: HOORAY – Can you tell us about some of your Adventures Sherlock Holmes ?

Sherlock :   Absolutely, I don't see why not – do you Watson?

Dr Watson: I don't see why not. They may sound familiar.

Sherlock : Elementary my dear Watson. Elementary

The Space Detectives and Sherlock Holmes

Narrator   Zip   Zap   Moriarty   Shop Keeper   Mrs Gossip
Sherlock Holmes   Watson

Narrator: Ladies and gentlemen, we present Scene 1- Somewhere deep in space

Sound effect: Noise of space ship then alarm

Zip: Captain, we have an emergency?

Zap: What is it?

Zip: Moriarty has escaped from prison.

Zap: Moriarty! He is the most dangerous criminal in the universe!

Zip: This is terrible.

Zap: Where is he?

Zip: Moriarty is on planet Earth.

Zap: We must go to planet Earth.

Zip, Zap: We are strong. We are clever.   We are …. The space detectives!

Sound effect: Space ship

Scene 2

Narrator: Scene 2 In a shop on planet Earth

Sound effect: **Door opening.**

Shop keeper: Hello, can I help you?

Mrs Gossip: Can I have a pear.

Shop keeper: A bear?

Mrs Gossip: No, a pear.

Shop keeper: You want a bear?

Mrs Gossip: No, no, a pear a pear.

Shop keeper: Anything else.

Mrs Gossip: Can I have a carrot?

Shop keeper: A parrot. I haven't got any parrots. This isn't a pet shop.

Mrs Gossip: A carrot, a carrot! I want a carrot!

Sound effect: **Door opening and footsteps**

Moriarty: Hands up!

Shopkeeper, Mrs Gossip: Ahhh!

Moriarty: Give me your money!

Mrs Gossip: Help, help! Call Sherlock Holmes

Shop keeper: Hello, Sherlock, there is a robber in the supermarket.

Sound effect: **Police siren, then footsteps.**

Sherlock Holmes and Watson: Don't panic, don't panic, we are ………… the super Investigators!

Sherlock Holmes: What is the problem?

Mrs Gossip: There is a robber.

Dr Watson: A robber? I see

Sherlock Holmes: What did he take?

Shopkeeper: He took our money.

Moriarty: Atchoo!

Sherlock: What was that?

Shopkeeper, Mrs Gossip: It´s the robber.

Sherlock Holmes: Hands up. He looks like someone we know Watson

Moriarty: You cannot stop me!

Dr Watson: Look at his hair…mmm yes…He looks like Moriarty… Let's catch him!!!!

Sound effect: Guns and lasers firing.

Sherlock Holmes: We can´t stop him

Dr Watson: He is too strong.

Moriarty: Ha, ha, ha. You cannot stop me! I am MORIARTY the Bad. No one can

stop me!

Sherlock Holmes and Dr Watson: Oh no! What are we going to do now??

Sound effect: Spaceship

Dr Watson: I say Sherlock…. What's that?

Shopkeeper, Mrs Gossip: It's a spaceship!

Sound effect: Spaceship door opening, then footsteps

Shopkeeper, Mrs Gossip, Sherlock: Who are you?

Zip, Zap: We are strong. We are clever.   We are …. The space detectives!

Shopkeeper, Mrs Gossip: There is a robber.

Zip: That's MORIARTY ---- the Bad!!

Zap: He is the most dangerous criminal in the universe!

Sound effect: Lasers firing.

Moriarty: You cannot stop me, I am strong, I am fast, I am ………….. err … dead!

Shopkeeper, Mrs Gossip: Hooray, hooray! You saved us.

Zip, Zap: You're welcome. The world is a safer place, thanks to …. The Space detectives!

Dr Watson : AND Sherlock Holmes of course!

Sherlock Holmes: Elementary my dear Watson….Elementary!!!!

The Treasure of Bolsena Island

Narrator   Sofia   Maria   Mattia   Captain Moriarty   Luca   Luisa   David

Scene 1

Narrator: Scene 1 In the town.

Sound effect: **People walking, bells ringing,**

Sofia: Hello, are you going shopping?

Maria: No, I haven't got any money. Have you got any money?

Mattia, Sofia: No, I haven't. Where can we get some money?

Maria: Look, what's that?

Mattia: It´s a map.

Sofia: It´s not just any old map – it is a treasure map.

Mattia: Look, X marks the spot where there is gold.

Maria: Where is the X – In fact Where is the gold?

Sofia: The X is near Lake Bolsena – that means the gold is on Bolsena Island.

Mattia, Maria: Fantastic! Let's go to Bolsena Island.

Scene 2

Narrator: Scene 2 On A pirate ship at lake Bolsena.

Sound effects: Seagulls and waves and singing a pirate song – Hooray and Up she rises, Hooray and Up she rises, Hooray and she rises early in the Morning

Luca:	Can you see the famous Bolsena island?
David:	No, I can't. Can you see the famous Bolsena island?
Luisa:	No I can't. Where is the island? Are you sure there is an Island?
Luca, David:	We must find the island.
Luisa:	We must find the gold.
Luca:	Look! I can see an island!
Captain Moriarty:	Give me the telescope!

Sound effects: Footsteps

Captain:	It's Bolsena Island. Let's go!

Scene 3

Narrator:	Scene 3 On Bolsena Island.

Sound effects: Seagull, waves, then footsteps.

Sofia:	Have you got the map?
Mattia:	Yes, I have got the map.
Maria:	Where is the gold?
Sofia:	It looks like the gold is in a big hole.

Mattia:	Can you see a big hole?
Maria:	No, I can't.
Sofia:	I can see a big cow under a tree. How strange! I thought we were on an Island…
Sound effect:	**Cows**
Maria:	I can see a small sheep next to a rock.
Sofia:	How Strange!!
Sound effect:	**Sheep**
Mattia:	I can see….
Maria, Sofia:	Yes?
Mattia:	I can see …. Captain Moriarty!
Maria, Sofia:	Captain Moriarty! OH NO They must be pirates! Oh no!
Mattia:	Let's hide behind this tree.
Sound effects:	**Footsteps.**
Luisa, Luca, David:	So where is the gold?
Captain Moriarty:	Don't worry. Luca, give me the map.
Luca:	What Map? I haven't got the map. You've got the map.
Captain Moriarty:	Don't be silly. I haven't got the map. You've got the map.
Everyone:	Who's got the map?
Maria:	Me!

Captain Moriarty:	Oh no they have got the map!
Luca, Luisa:	Stop them! They have got the map.
Mattia, Sofia, Maria:	Ahhhhhh!! Quick Run…
Sound effect:	**They all run around in circles.**
Captain Moriarty:	Hands up!
Mattia, Sofia, Maria:	Oh no!
Captain Moriarty:	Give me the map! Look X marks the spot and the gold is in a big hole.
Luca:	Look! Captain, there is a big hole.
Luisa:	Let's look in the big hole.
Sound effect:	**Running sounds**
Sofia:	What are we going to do?
Mattia:	I have got an idea.
Jane:	What is it?
Mattia:	Push the pirates into the hole.
Mattia, Sofia, Maria:	Ok, push after 3 - 1, 2 AND 3 - HOOOOORAY
Pirates:	Ahhhhhhhhhh!
Sound effect:	Big crash and bang as pirates land in the hole
Pirates:	Help, help!
Maria:	If you must give us the gold, then we will let you out.
Captain Moriarty:	Ok. OK = we give up – let us out of here - Here you are.
Sofia:	Here - Climb up this rope.

Pirates: Thank you, thank you.

Maria, Sofia, Mattia: Are you going to be on your best behaviour – and Be Kind and good pirates?

Pirates: Yes. We Promise

Everyone: Ok then - Let's have a big party. Hooray! Hooray!

Everyone: The end.

Sherlock Holmes and the case of the mummy

*Sherlock Holmes   Dr Watson   Moriarty   Peter   Sally
Max   Mummy   Narrator*

Narrator: Ladies and gentlemen, we present Sherlock Holmes and the case of the Mummy. Scene 1 in the museum

Sound effect: Rain, thunder and lightning. Door opening and footsteps.

Sally, Peter, Max: (children looking around) Where are we?

Moriarty: Shhh!!! We are in the museum.

Max: What´s that?

Moriarty: It´s a mummy.

Sally: This is the mummy of Ramses. He was an Egyptian Pharaoh.

Peter: What is this book?

Moriarty: This is the Book of the Dead.

Sally: Can you read it?

Moriarty: Of course. It says "Impum impum oestrum neenum!"

Mummy: Errrrrrr! *(groaning)*

Peter, Max: What´s that?

Sally: I don´t know.

Max, Sally, Peter: Aaahh!! Look! The mummy. It's moving!

Mummy: I am King Ramses, I am King Ramses, I am..

Moriarty: Stop! I am your master!

Mummy: You are my master!

Max, Sally, Peter: Wow! The book controls the mummy.

Sound effect: Alarm

Max, Sally, Peter: Oh no, quick, let´s go.

Narrator: Later that night, Sherlock Holmes arrives.

Sound effect: Footsteps.

Sherlock: We have to find the mummy, Watson.

Dr Watson: This is a mystery, Holmes.

Sherlock: Let´s look for some clues.

Dr Watson: There is some mud and hay on the floor.

Sherlock: Aha! The robbers live on a farm. Follow me Watson.

Sound effect: Footsteps running, car engine starts then drives off.

Scene 2

Narrator: Scene 2, in the countryside.

Sound effect: Cows, sheep, horses etc. Then car, then footsteps.

Dr Watson: Where are we Holmes?

Sherlock: This is a farm. Professor Moriarty lives here.

Dr Watson: Who is Professor Moriarty?

Sherlock: Professor Moriarty is a farmer who collects Egyptian things.

Moriarty: Can I help you?

Sherlock: Hello, Professor Moriarty. Have you seen a mummy?

Moriarty: No, I haven´t.

Sound effect: Cows

Mummy: Errrrr!

Dr Watson: What was that?

Peter: Err… nothing. The cow is ill.

Sound effect: Sheep

Mummy: Errrrr!

Dr Watson: What was that?

Sally, Max: Er… nothing. The sheep is ill.

Mummy: Errr!!! I am King Rameses.

Dr Watson: It´s the mummy!

Moriarty: Quick, let´s go to my secret castle.

Sound effect: Footsteps, then car drives off.

Scene 3, Moriarty's secret castle

Sound effect: thunder, lightning

Moriarty: Welcome to my castle.

Sound effect: Door opening and footsteps.

Moriarty: With the Book of the Dead, no one can stop me, ha, ha, ha!

Sherlock: Not so fast, Moriarty!

Sherlock: Watson, get the book.

Moriarty: Rameses, stop Sherlock Holmes.

Mummy: As you command! Errrhh! Stop! I am King Rameses.

Sound effect: Footsteps

Watson: Give me the book!

Sound effect: Big fight

Watson: I have got the book, Holmes. " Imana bidana ipsum delvum"

Mummy: I am King Rameses, I am, I am, I am sleepy……. zzzzzzz

Sherlock: Hands up Professor Moriarty!

Max, Peter, Sally: Oh no! We surrender.

Watson: You are going to prison.

Moriarty: I will return, Sherlock Holmes, I will return!

Everyone: The end.

Sherlock Holmes in The Playground

Cast: Miss Asia, Irene, Anna, Chiara, Elena, Elisa, Lorenzo, Aurora, Sherlock Holmes, Watson

Scene 1

(In the Playground the children play and Miss Asia drinks her tea.)

Lorenzo: Come and see what we have found?

Irene : We think you will like it.

(Elisa, Anna, Elena and Aurora drop their skipping ropes and walk to Irene and Chiara)

Elisa: What is it?

Elena: I hope it's exciting.

Anna: Quick let's see – it sounds exciting

Aurora : I bet it is a box of sweets

Chiara: I wonder what it is…

(Lorenzo places a big worm in their hands)

Elena: *(Screaming)* That's disgusting.

Elisa: It feels all slimy.

Irene : It is very cute. Don't hurt it!

Lorenzo: Look, there are loads of them.

Anna: We could make a worm pie.

Chiara: I wouldn't want to eat worms, even if there was no other food in the world.

Aurora: We wouldn't really eat them, just pretend!

Elena: *(Smiling)* I see.

Lorenzo: Shall we show Miss Asia?

Aurora: Nah, she'll probably tell us off.

Elisa: Why? We haven't done anything wrong.

Chiara: Yeah, we haven't hurt them.

Lorenzo: Well what shall we do then?

Anna :   Put it under that stone.

(Sherlock and Watson arrive at the school)

Sherlock : Good morning Children

Watson : How is everyone today?

Children : Hello Sherlock and Dr Watson... we are fine thank you?

Sherlock : What are you all doing out here?

Lorenzo : We are discovering new things ...like WORMS

Watson : I see Worms – Very interesting

Miss Asia : They are all having fun out here, it is their break time...although it is over now...

Miss Asia : Come on Children, Playtime is over. It is time to go back to the class everyone.

Chiara : Can we please play for 5 more minutes?

Lorenzo : We have found something, come and see…

Miss Asia : What have you found?

Anna : Oh, it is just some rocks and leaves

Aurora : Yes, it is nothing special

Elisa : Well…it is just a stone

Elena: Yes, look a small pretty stone

Sherlock : it looks very big to me, more like a Rock

Watson : Why don't you look underneath it, maybe there are some worms

Miss Asia : Yes, maybe there are some worms and ants and bugs

Irene : I will lift the stone very carefully

Lorenzo : I am so excited, I bet you will find lots of worms

(Irene turned over the stone and everyone gasped)

Everyone : Oh no, oh no, be careful

Miss Asia : Stop worrying. Worms can't hurt you

(turning over the stone)

Everyone : WOOOOOOOW

Elena : Look – Wow

Aurora : Oh my goodness, oh my goodness

Anna : WOW, it is a beautiful Yellow Butterfly

Everyone : WOW, it is so pretty

Lorenzo : And look there is a worm too

Chiara : And a Ladybird

Elisa : Even some Ants

Aurora : Nature is so beautiful

Miss Asia : Yes it is and that is why we must look after all of the beautiful things around us.

Anna : We are so lucky Miss Asia to learn about Nature

Elena : Yes, and even in our very own playground

Everyone : We must be kind and gentle as all of these beautiful creatures can teach us so much about Respect for each other and for our beautiful world.

Everyone : YES, KINDNESS ALWAYS WINS! HOORAY!!!

Sherlock : Elementary my dear children Elementary

SHERLOCK MEETS THE CAPITANO DEL POPOLO

CHARACTERS: NARRATOR, CAPITANO DEL POPOLO SOLDIERS, SHERLOCK, MARKET TRADERS 1,2,3,4. WITCH

NARRATOR: A long time ago, the Capitano di Popolo was captured while he was hunting in the Tuscan land.

SOLDIERS: Stop! You are not allowed to hunt in our Tuscan land. Who gave you permission?

CAPITANO: Nobody.

SOLDIERS: Then you must come with us. We will take you to Sherlock Holmes who will INVESTIGATE YOU (WINK WINK)

NARRATOR: When Sherlock Holmes saw him, he was surprised

Sherlock: You are an imposter – You are from UMBRIA - I know who you are- YOU ARE the Capitano di Popolo from Orvieto

CAPITANO: But How did you know that?

Sherlock: I can see that you are strong character, and possibly a great Swordsperson. It is the way you walk with excellence.

CAPITANO: Why thank you very much for the compliment (Bowing his head)

Sherlock: I will give you one hour to find out the answer to a very difficult question.

CAPITANO: What is the question?

Sherlock: What is the Orvieto Diamond?.

CAPITANO: That is an impossible question to answer. But my life is worth it, I will give you the answer.

Sherlock: You are free to go. And don´t forget, I´ll be waiting for you.

CAPITANO: I will BE back.

NARRATOR: Capitano di popolo returned to Orvieto and started questioning everybody. The princess, the queen, the priests, the wisemen, but no one had an answer. Then he asked one of the market people.

THE MARKET SCENE :

People singing, juggling, playing and selling…

M1 – Apples for Sale

M2 – Come buy my fruit and vegetables

M3 – My sweet red tomatoes

M4 – Oranges apples lemons and strawberries

CAPITANO : Excuse Me – But do you know What the Orvieto Diamond is ?

M1, 2, 3, 4 – NO – Never heard of it before

Market owners: Well, people say there´s a witch living in the deep forest. They say that she is very smart, but evil. Why don´t you go and ask her?

CAPITANO: The princess, and the queen also suggested that I should see her.

M1: Then you must do it.

M2: Don´t go alone, take some soldiers with you. She´s not very nice.

NARRATOR: That same night the Capitano went to the old witch´s house.

WITCH: I have been expecting you. I know that your time is running out.

CAPITANO: If you already know why I´m here, then tell me the answer.

WITCH: Show me your skills as a swordsperson and show person and maybe I will tell you what the Diamond is.

Narrator : Capitano danced with the sword in true Orvietan style. The crowds watched. Sherlock watched from a distance.

Sherlock: I say….What a great talent you have ! Did you find me the answer about the diamond?

CAPITANO: No, I am sorry, but it is impossible

Sherlock: My dear Capitano – IT IS YOU

CAPITANO: Me? What do you mean?

Sherlock: It is Elementary my dear Capitano - Elementary!

YOU ARE THE DIAMOND OF ORVIETO – The one who can show his talents and believes in himself is a TRUE Diamond

CAPITANO: WOW – YES It is true – WE ARE ALL DIAMONDS and WE MUST SHINE BRIGHT LIKE A DIAMOND

(singing Bright like a diamond in the sky…)

Everyone : HOORAY! And WE ALL lived happily ever after in our little city on the rock - ORVIETO

Sherlock Holmes meets the Monster of Orvieto

Narrator, Sherlock Holmes, Watson, Doctor Frankenstein, Monster, Sarah, Policewoman, man (small part 1 line)

Scene 1

Narrator: Ladies and gentlemen, we present..."The Monster of Orvieto" Scene 1, in the forest.

Sound effect: Wind, rain

(Sherlock and Watson enter)

Sherlock: Where is Doctor Frankenstein's castle?

Watson: I don't know. I think we are lost.

Sherlock: Look, there is a man.

Sound effect: Footsteps

Watson: Excuse me, where is Doctor Frankenstein's castle?

Man: Doctor Frankenstein's castle, don't go there, don't go there! Aaahh!!!!

Sound effect: **Footsteps**

Sherlock: Look! A door!

Sound effect: **Doorbell then door opening**

Doctor Frankenstein: Hello, can I help you?

Sherlock: My name is Sherlock Holmes, I am your new gardener. (wink wink)

Watson: My name is Watson. I'm your new cook.(wink wink)

Doctor Frankenstein: Excellent, excellent, please come in.

Sound effect: **Door closing**

Doctor Frankenstein: Welcome to my castle.

Watson: What's this?

Doctor Frankenstein: This is my laboratory.

Sherlock: What's this?

Doctor Frankenstein: This is my new experiment.

Sherlock and Watson: Huh!!!!!!!!

Doctor Frankenstein: And it is finished. Watch this!

(Doctor Frankenstein presses a button but the monster doesn't move)

Sound effect: Electrical noises, buzzing etc

Doctor Frankenstein: Oh dear. Nothing happened

Sherlock and Watson: I'm tired.

Doctor Frankenstein: Lets' go to bed and we'll try again tomorrow.

Sound effect: Footsteps

Narrator: Later that night.

Sound effect: Footsteps

Watson: I say Sherlock, What's this?

Sherlock: Don't touch it Watson!

Sound effect: Electrical noises, buzzing etc

Monster: Grrrhhhh!!!!!!

Sherlock: Oh no!

Watson: The monster is escaping!

Sherlock: Oh no…You fool Watson !

Sound effect: Footsteps

Sherlock, Watson: We have to catch him. Call the police for extra help.

Watson: Hello, police, please come quickly, there is an escaped monster.

Scene 2

Narrator: Scene 2. in the forest.

Sound effect: **Birds**

Sarah: Ah .... what a beautiful day.

Monster: Grrrhhh!!!!!

Sound effect: **Footsteps**

Sarah: Ahhhh. A monster!

Monster: Grrhh!! I am not a monster, I am ....f....f.....f..... friend.

Sarah: What's your name?

Monster: My....my...my....n...n....n...name?

Sarah: Yes, what .....is.......your........ name?

Monster: My name is ...monster.

Sound effect: **Police siren**

Policewoman: Stop! This is the police!

Monster: Grrrhhh!!!!!

Policewoman: It's a monster.

Sound effect: **Footsteps**

Sarah: He isn't a monster. He is good. He wants to be our friend.

Monster: Monster ... f...f....f...friend.

Doctor Frankenstein: Hooray, my experiment is a success.

Monster: Monster is hungry.

Sherlock: Well, let's have a party then!!!

Everyone: Hooray.

LITTLE RED RIDING HOOD MEETS SHERLOCK HOLMES

Mum, Little Red Riding hood, Wolf, Sherlock Holmes, Watson, Grandma

Scene 1 At Little Red Riding Hood's home

MUM : Good morning my lovely daughter Little Red Riding Hood.

RED : Good Morning, Mum!

MUM : Look, I made a cake for Grandma. Can you take it to her?

RED : Yes Mum, Of course Mmm! Yummy! I will Put it in the basket, please, and go to Grandma's.

MUM : Make sure you stay on the path – do not go into the forest ?

RED : Ok Mum. Bye, bye!

RED : It's a beautiful day. Look at the flowers! So many flowers – Roses are Red, Violets are blue – Oh look – Daffodils – These Flowers are so beautiful I must take some for Grandma!

WOLF : Hello! Hello! What's your name, little girl?

RED : My name's Little Red Riding Hood. What's your name?

WOLF : I'm a Big Bad Wolf! What's in your basket, Little Red Riding Hood?

RED : It is a cake for Grandma! My Mummy made it for her

WOLF : Mmm! Yummy!

RED : Bye, bye, Big Bad Wolf! I must go now - I am not allowed to talk to strangers

WOLF : Bye, bye, Little Red Riding Hood!

SHERLOCK HOLMES IS GOING FOR A WALK WITH WATSON

SHERLOCK : I say Watson, did you see that?

WATSON : Do you mean did I see that wolf talking to Little Red Riding Hood. ? Yes I did

SHERLOCK : Well, we all know the story…Let's go and INVSETIGATE

WOLF : Hello, Grandma! I have come to EAT you and I am going to EAT Little RED too…HA HA HAAAAA!

GRANDMA : Aargh! A wolf! Help!

THE WOLF EATS GRANDMA AND GETS INTO THE BED.

SHERLOCK AND HOLMES ARRIVE

SHERLOCK : Knock Knock

Wolf : Please come in …

SHERLOCK : Hello dear Grandma with the Big Teeth

Wolf : Where is little Red ?

Watson : We saw you talking to her so we thought we would interrupt your story

Sherlock : Well – you weren't expecting that were you?

Little RED Arrives at Grandma's House

Red : Hello, Grandma!

Sherlock : Hello, Little Red Riding Hood! How are you?

RED : Sherlock Holmes – What are you doing here ?

Sherlock : Oh... we want you to see some clues …

Watson : Yes – there is someone who is very bad!

Red : Grandma, what big eyes you have!

Wolf : Yes! All the better to see you!

Sherlock : UM…Yes the story goes like that…

Red : Grandma, what big ears you have !

Wolf : Yes! All the better to hear you with my dear!

Red : Grandma, what a big nose you have!

Wolf : Yes! All the better to smell you with!

Red : But Grandma, what big teeth you have!

Wolf : Yes! All the better to eat you with!

Sherlock : Ok OK Let's stop there shall we ?

Watson : Little Red riding hood – Do you know who this is?

Red : Aaargh!! Help! Help! It's the wolf!

Wolf : Yes I'm the big bad wolf!

Sherlock : Well that was easy – Come on Wolfy, you are coming

with

us..

Watson : Yes – Come along dear wolfy and you can take Grandma out of your tummy before we call the Woodcutter to do it for you… You decide!

Wolf – Ok ok – here she is…

(Grandma jumps out from behind the Wolf)

RED : Thank you Sherlock Holmes! Thank you!

Grandma : Yes Thank you Sherlock Holmes – how did you know I was in there?

Sherlock : Elementary my dear Grandma, Elementary!!!

Watson : you did it again Sherlock –

What a fairytale ending!!!

Sherlock : I say Watson, don't we always end with a party?

EVERYONE : Yes, let's have a party! HURRAY!

Printed in Dunstable, United Kingdom